The Essentials of

Meatless Pizza

Pizza for Vegetarians

By

Angel Burns

License Notices

Get Your Daily Deals Here!

Free books on me! Subscribe now to receive free and discounted books directly to your email. This means you will always have choices of your next book from the comfort of your own home and a reminder email will pop up a few days beforehand, so you never miss out! Every day, free books will make their way into your inbox and all you need to do is choose what you want.

What could be better than that?

Fill out the box below to get started on this amazing offer and start receiving your daily deals right away!

https://angel-burns.gr8.com

Table of Contents

Delicious Vegetarian Pizza Recipes

HHHHHHHHHHHHHHHHHHHHHHHHHHHHHHHHHHHHHHHH

Recipe 1: Greek Pita Pizzas

This recipe is another dish that uses small individual-sized pitas as the base for the pizza instead of pizza crusts. My kids love loading these tasty treats up with their favorite toppings and then watch as they bake to a golden brown.

Total Prep Time: 20 minutes

Yield: 2

Ingredient List:

- 1 ounce lemon juice
- ½ tsp. garlic powder
- ¼ tsp. oregano, dried
- ¼ tsp. basil, dried
- 3 ounces extra-virgin olive oil
- 2 x 4" pita bread rounds
- 16 ounces fresh spinach, torn
- 2 ounces grape tomatoes, cut in half
- 1 ½ ounces green olives with pimentos, chopped
- 4 ounces mozzarella cheese, shredded
- 4 ounces feta cheese, crumbled

HHHHHHHHHHHHHHHHHHHHHHHHHHHHHHHHHHHHHHH

[9]

Instructions:

1. Preheat oven to 375 degrees Fahrenheit

2. Combine lemon juice, garlic, oregano and basil in a small bowl until all Ingredients are blended together

3. Arrange pitas on a baking sheet and brush lightly with ½ ounce of the mixture from the bowl

4. In a separate bowl; toss spinach, tomatoes and olives together

5. Pour the rest of the contents from the bowl on the vegetables and toss until completed coated

6. Spread mixture over the pitas evenly and then top with mozzarella and feta cheese

7. Bake for 8 minutes or until pitas are lightly browned and cheese is melted

Recipe 2: Goat Cheese and Tomato Pizza

I am new to using goat cheese on my pizzas, but I find that the sharp taste of this cheese is a natural complement to the other Ingredients. I will often serve this pizza with some hot sauce either drizzled over or on the side of this dish.

Total Prep Time: 20 minutes

Yield: 8

Ingredient List:

- 6 ounces tomato paste
- 6 ounces water
- 2 ounces extra-virgin olive oil
- ½ ounce Italian seasoning
- ½ tsp. garlic salt
- 1/8 tsp. cayenne pepper
- ½ tsp. black pepper, ground
- 2 diced plum tomatoes
- 13 ounces dry pizza crust mix
- 6 thinly sliced plum tomatoes
- 4 ounces crumbled goat cheese

HHHHHHHHHHHHHHHHHHHHHHHHHHHHHHHHHHHHHHHH

Instructions:

1. Preheat oven to 400 degrees Fahrenheit

2. Combine tomato paste, water, and oil in a small saucepan and stir well

3. Add garlic salt, seasoning, and both peppers

4. Simmer for 20 minutes on Low

5. Grease a baking sheet or pizza pan and spread the pizza dough on the pan following the instructions on the package

6. Spread tomato paste mixture evenly over the pizza crust

7. Arrange tomatoes and goat cheese over the sauce and bake for 15 minutes or until cheese melts and crust is golden brown

Recipe 3: Garden Vegetable Pizza

Crescent roll dough melts in your mouth when combined with the pizza Ingredients in this recipe. I try to use this flaky dough often when I am entertaining because it creates a unique consistency that you don't usually find in regular pizza.

Total Prep Time: 5 minutes

Yield: 24

Ingredient List:

- 8 ounces refrigerated crescent rolls
- 8 ounces softened cream cheese
- 1 ounce dry Ranch dressing mix
- 2 finely chopped carrots
- 4 ounces red bell peppers, chopped
- 4 ounces green bell pepper, chopped
- 4 ounces broccoli, chopped
- 4 ounces green onions, chopped

HHHHHHHHHHHHHHHHHHHHHHHHHHHHHHHHHHHHHHH

Instructions:

1. Preheat oven to 375 degrees Fahrenheit

2. On a non-stick baking sheet, roll out the crescent roll dough until it is a large triangle in the middle of the baking sheet

3. Bake for 13 minutes or until golden brown. Remove from heat and set it aside

4. Mix cream cheese and ½ ounce of Ranch dressing mix in a bowl

5. Spread the cream cheese over the crescent roll crust

6. Add the rest of the Ingredients and then put the pizza in the refrigerator for 1 hour

7. Cut into small squares and serve

Recipe 4: Eggplant Pistachio Pizza

The beautiful thing about vegetarian pizzas is that any combination of **Ingredient List:** can be baked together to create a delicious meal. This eggplant pistachio pizza recipe is no exception as it contains many untraditional elements that blend to form perfection.

Total Prep Time: 15 minutes

Yield: 4

Ingredient List:

- 12 ounces pizza dough
- 1 medium eggplant, cut lengthwise into 6 thin strips
- 2 ounces Extra-virgin olive oil
- Kosher salt
- Red-pepper flakes
- 4 ounces chopped salted pistachios
- 2 ½ ounces feta, crumbled
- 2 ½ ounces pomegranate seeds
- 2 ounces cilantro leaves, lightly packed

HHHHHHHHHHHHHHHHHHHHHHHHHHHHHHHHHHHHHHH

Instructions:

1. Preheat oven to 475 degrees Fahrenheit.

2. Spread dough out on a rectangular baking sheet, covering the entire sheet

3. Arrange eggplant on the dough evenly in 6 evenly spaced slices

4. Drizzle with olive oil and sprinkle with flakes and salt

5. Bake for 18 minutes or until crust is golden brown

6. Place pizza on a flat serving dish and add pistachios, feta and pomegranate evenly over the top

7. Season with cilantro before serving

Recipe 5: Spinach Pizza

This recipe looks like a pie with some delicious spinach filling, but I still refer to it as a pizza. The crust is light and flaky and tastes fantastic when you take a bite of this tasty meal.

Total Prep Time: 10 minutes

Yield: 4

Ingredient List:

- 2 x 9" refrigerated pie crusts
- 1 ounce olive oil
- 1 chopped onion
- 16 ounces thawed frozen spinach, drained and chopped
- 15 ounces ricotta cheese
- 16 ounces mozzarella cheese, shredded and divided
- 1 ounce Parmesan cheese, grated
- ½ tsp. salt
- ½ tsp. black pepper, ground

HHHHHHHHHHHHHHHHHHHHHHHHHHHHHHHHHHHHHHHH

Instructions:

1. Take the pie crusts out of the packaging and set aside

2. Preheat oven to 450 degrees Fahrenheit

3. Heat oil in a large frying pan on medium heat

4. Sauté onion in the oil for 3 minutes or until translucent

5. Stir in spinach and cook for 2 minutes until liquid has evaporated

6. Remove the onion and spinach from the pan and let them cool

7. In a large bowl, mix ricotta, 12 ounces of mozzarella, parmesan, salt and pepper together. Add spinach and mix

8. Put a pie crust on a baking sheet and smooth out any fold lines with your fingers

9. Spread half of the Ingredients from bowl onto the pie crust, leaving 1" clean from the edge

10. Fold the edge of the pie crust over the toppings and then repeat the same thing with the other one

11. Sprinkle the remaining 4 ounces of mozzarella over the two pies and bake for 20 minutes or until golden brown

Recipe 6: Pesto Pizza

Pesto sauce is a lovely alternative to the traditional tomato sauce pizza base. The fresh peppers and tomatoes taste divine when combined with the olives and artichokes in this simple and delicious recipe.

Total Prep Time: 10 minutes

Yield: 6

Ingredient List:

- 12" prepared pizza crust
- 4 ounces pesto
- 1 chopped tomato, ripened
- 4 ounces chopped green bell pepper
- 2 ounces chopped black olives
- ½ chopped red onion
- 4 ounces canned and sliced artichoke hearts, drained
- 8 ounces feta cheese, crumbled

HHHHHHHHHHHHHHHHHHHHHHHHHHHHHHHHHHHHHH

Instructions:

1. Preheat oven to 450 degrees Fahrenheit

2. Put pizza crust on a large baking sheet or pizza stone and spread the pizza evenly over top

3. Add the rest of the Ingredients in whichever order you decide

4. Bake for 10 minutes or until cheese is melted and bubbly

Recipe 7: Provolone and Cherry Tomato Pizza

If you want to add a unique taste to this pizza recipe, then you can also add some smoked salmon to the top that will complement the capers and cherry tomatoes. The lettuce gives this dish a crunchy consistency that everyone will enjoy.

Total Prep Time: 15 minutes

Yield: 4

Ingredient List:

- 24 ounces of torn arugula
- 16 ounces thinly sliced radicchio
- ½ ounce drained capers, packed in vinegar
- ¼ tsp. red-pepper flakes
- ½ ounce extra-virgin olive oil
- 12 ounces pizza dough
- 6 slices provolone
- 10 cherry tomatoes, cut in half
- Kosher salt

HHHHHHHHHHHHHHHHHHHHHHHHHHHHHHHHHHHHHHHH

Instructions:

1. Preheat oven to 475 degrees Fahrenheit

2. Add arugula, radicchio, capers, pepper flakes and olive oil in a bowl and toss until fully coated

3. In a rectangular baking sheet, spread dough until it covers the sheet

4. Place provolone on the dough evenly and then add the arugula mixture

5. Bake for 22 minutes or until crust is golden brown

6. Add cherry tomatoes and salt before serving

Recipe 8: Greek Pizza

This Mediterranean style pizza has quite a few Ingredients that combined make the unique and delicious Greek pizza I have ever tasted. Try serving this recipe with some tzatziki on the side for dipping.

Total Prep Time: 20 minutes

Yield: 4

Ingredient List:

- ½ ounce extra-virgin olive oil
- 4 ounces onion, diced
- 2 minced cloves garlic
- 10 ounces thawed frozen spinach, chopped (squeeze excess juice out)
- 2 ounces basil, chopped
- 2 ¼ tsp. lemon juice
- 1 ½ tsp. oregano, dried
- A pinch of black pepper, ground
- 14 ounces refrigerated pizza crust
- ½ ounce olive oil
- 16 ounces mozzarella cheese, shredded and divided
- 1 thinly sliced tomato
- 2 ½ ounces Italian seasoned bread crumbs
- 6 ounces feta cheese, crumbled

HHHHHHHHHHHHHHHHHHHHHHHHHHHHHHHHHHHHHHH

[30]

Instructions:

1. Preheat oven to 400 degrees Fahrenheit.

2. Heat ½ ounce of oil in a large frying pan

3. Sauté onion and garlic in the oil for 5 minutes or until onion is translucent and garlic is tender

4. Stir in spinach and continue to cook for 7 minutes or until liquid is gone

5. Remove from heat and sprinkle the spinach mixture with lemon juice, basil, oregano and pepper

6. Spread pizza dough out on a pizza stone or baking sheet

7. Brush with ½ ounce of oil and spread the spinach mixture evenly over the crust, leaving some space around the edges

8. Sprinkle 8 ounces of mozzarella over the spinach

9. arrange tomatoes and bread crumbs evenly over the pizza and then top with 8 ounces of mozzarella and all of the feta cheese

10. Bake for 15 minutes or until crust is lightly browned and cheese is melted

Recipe 9: Pepper and Red Onion Pizza

If you want to make this pizza spicier, then you can substitute regular bell peppers for roasted or spicy peppers. I like to cut this pizza into small squares and serve as an appetizer at gatherings with a side of ranch dressing for dipping.

Total Prep Time: 30 minutes

Yield: 4

Ingredient List:

- 2 red bell peppers, cut lengthwise into 8 slices
- 1 red onion, sliced into ½" round pieces
- 2 ounces extra-virgin olive oil, divided
- 6 ounces of room temperature goat cheese
- 6 ounces Parmesan, finely grated
- 1 tsp. lemon zest
- 1 tsp. lemon juice
- 16 ounces prepared pizza dough, separated into 4 x 4 ounces pieces
- a pinch of salt and pepper
- 8 ounces arugula
- Red-pepper flakes

HHHHHHHHHHHHHHHHHHHHHHHHHHHHHHHHHHHHHHHH

Instructions:

1. Heat half of the oil in a large frying pan on medium high heat

2. Add peppers and onion to the oil and cook for 10 minutes, tossing frequently

3. Stir in goat cheese, parmesan cheese, lemon zest, lemon juice and the rest of the oil

4. Grease a rimmed pizza pan or baking sheet with olive oil and spread the dough out until it covers the whole sheet

5. Lightly brush the crust with oil and sprinkle with salt

6. Bake the crust for 2 minutes and remove from heat

7. Arrange cheese mixture over the crust evenly

8. Mix arugula in a small bowl with lemon juice and olive oil. Sprinkle salt and pepper in the bowl and then toss to fully coat the arugula

9. Add arugula and red-pepper flakes to the pizza

Recipe 10: Veggie Delight Pizza

This pizza is a purely vegetarian dish that uses a handful of Ingredients to create a tasty and nutritious dinner for the whole family. I like to make a few of these and freeze one for a future meal where I may be short on time.

Total Prep Time: 20 minutes

Yield: 2

Ingredient List:

- 12" prepared pizza crust
- 1 ounce extra-virgin olive oil
- 9 ounces tomato sauce, seasoned
- 4 ounces onion, sliced
- 8 ounces fresh mushrooms, sliced
- 4 ounces green bell pepper, chopped
- 2 ounces black olives, chopped
- 16 ounces mozzarella cheese, shredded

HHHHHHHHHHHHHHHHHHHHHHHHHHHHHHHHHHHHHHHH

Instructions:

1. Preheat the oven to 350 degrees Fahrenheit

2. Put the pizza crust on a large baking sheet or pizza stone and brush lightly with olive oil

3. Spread tomato sauce over the oil, then arrange the onion, mushrooms, peppers and olives on the sauce

4. Top with the mozzarella cheese and bake for 12 minutes or until cheese has melted

Recipe 11: Puff Pastry Pizza

The pastry shell creates a soft and chewy base for this tasty vegetarian pizza recipe. I enjoy the mixture of tastes formed by the combination of gorgonzola and mozzarella cheese.

Total Prep Time: 20 minutes

Yield: 16

Ingredient List:

- 17 ¼ ounces of thawed frozen puff pastry sheets
- 1 ounce extra virgin olive oil
- 3 thinly sliced green onions
- ½ ounce white onion, diced
- 1 minced clove of garlic
- 6 chopped sun-dried tomatoes
- 2 tsp. rosemary, dried
- 16 ounces mozzarella cheese, shredded
- 2 ounces Gorgonzola cheese, crumbled

HHHHHHHHHHHHHHHHHHHHHHHHHHHHHHHHHHHHHH

[39]

Instructions:

1. Preheat oven to 400 degrees Fahrenheit

2. Put sheets of pastry on a large baking sheet and pinch the two together so it makes one large piece of pastry

3. Bake for 15 minutes

4. Heat oil in a small frying pan on medium heat

5. Add onions, garlic, tomatoes and rosemary to the olive oil and cook for 5 minutes or until onions are tender

6. Remove the pastry from heat and sprinkle mozzarella cheese and Gorgonzola over the top of the crust

7. Arrange onion and garlic mixture evenly over the cheese and bake for 10 minutes or until cheese is melted

Recipe 12: Pear and Gorgonzola Pizza

The sweetness of the pear tastes terrific when paired with the Gorgonzola cheese. I love blue cheese on a pizza, and I serve this with some hot sauce like Frank's for those who enjoy a little kick with their food.

Total Prep Time: 10 minutes

Yield: 8

Ingredient List:

- 16 ounces refrigerated pizza crust
- 4 ounces provolone cheese, thinly sliced
- 1 thinly sliced pear
- 2 ounces walnuts, chopped
- 2 ½ ounces crumbled Gorgonzola cheese
- 1 ounce fresh chives, chopped

HHHHHHHHHHHHHHHHHHHHHHHHHHHHHHHHHHHHHHH

Instructions:

1. Preheat the oven to 450 degrees Fahrenheit

2. Spread pizza crust dough out on a large baking sheet or pizza stone

3. Add Provolone, then the pear slices, then the Gorgonzola in layers

4. Bake for 10 minutes or until cheese has been melted and the crust is golden brown

5. Sprinkle pizza with chives before serving

Recipe 13: Portobello Mushroom Pizza

You can substitute other types of meaty mushrooms if you are unable to find Portobellos, but I prefer these beefy fungi when I make this pizza. I have also loaded on the goat cheese much more than this recipe suggests because I love the stuff!

Total Prep Time: 10 minutes

Yield: 8

[43]

Ingredient List:

- 10 ounces refrigerated pizza crust dough
- ½ ounce olive oil
- 2 minced cloves of garlic
- 1 sliced red bell pepper
- 1 sliced yellow bell pepper
- 2 thinly sliced portobello mushrooms
- 6 ½ ounces marinated artichoke hearts, chopped
- 4 ounces crumbled goat cheese
- 1 ½ ounces balsamic vinegar

HHHHHHHHHHHHHHHHHHHHHHHHHHHHHHHHHHHHHHH

Instructions:

1. Preheat the oven to 350 degrees Fahrenheit

2. Spray a pizza pan with cooking spray

3. Spread the dough on the pizza pan and lightly brush with olive oil

4. Disperse the garlic over the pizza crust, and then arrange the bell peppers, mushrooms and artichokes over the garlic

5. Top with goat cheese and some balsamic vinegar

6. Bake for 20 minutes or until crust is golden brown

Recipe 14: Mushroom Pizza

You can also put this pizza under the broiler for a minute or two to reduce any excess liquid created by the mushrooms. The combination of spinach, mushrooms, and mozzarella produces a tasty and hearty meal you will make many times for years to come.

Total Prep Time: 10 minutes

Yield: 8

Ingredient List:

- 12" prepared pizza crust
- 1 ½ ounces extra-virgin olive oil
- 1 tsp. sesame oil
- 8 ounces rinsed spinach, squeeze dried
- 8 ounces mozzarella cheese, shredded
- 8 ounces fresh mushrooms, sliced

HHHHHHHHHHHHHHHHHHHHHHHHHHHHHHHHHHHHHHH

Instructions:

1. Preheat oven to 350 degrees Fahrenheit

2. Put pizza crust on a large baking sheet or pizza pan

3. Combine olive oil and sesame oil in a small mixing bowl

4. Brush the pizza crust with the mixture from the bowl evenly

5. Add a layer of spinach, then mozzarella, then mushrooms

6. Bake for 10 minutes until cheese has been melted and the crust is golden brown

Recipe 15: Sage and Apple Sausage

The vegetarian sausage used in this recipe creates a meaty consistency that provides a filling and hearty meal for the whole family. I like to use these meat substitutes for pizzas because they allow for an exciting taste when mixed with the rest of the Ingredients.

Total Prep Time: 10 minutes

Yield: 4

Ingredient List:

- 2 tsp. olive oil
- 8 ounces sweet onion, sliced thin
- 12" prepared thin pizza crust
- 4 ounces pizza sauce
- 2 sliced vegetarian sage and apple sausages (made by Yves Cuisine)
- 2 sliced strips of vegetarian bacon
- 4 ounces orange, yellow and red bell peppers, sliced
- 1 ounce Parmesan cheese, grated
- 6 ounces mozzarella cheese, shredded

HHHHHHHHHHHHHHHHHHHHHHHHHHHHHHHHHHHHHH

Instructions:

1. Preheat oven to 400 degrees Fahrenheit

2. Heat olive oil in a large frying pan on medium low heat

3. Sauté onion in the oil for 7 minutes, stirring frequently

4. Remove from heat and set aside

5. Put the pizza crust on a pizza pan and spread the pizza sauce evenly over top

6. Add vegetarian sausage and bacon, peppers and onions

7. Top with parmesan and mozzarella cheeses

8. Bake for 10 minutes or until cheese has been melted and the crust is golden brown

Recipe 16: Butternut Squash Pizza

I would have never thought of adding squash to pizza until
I tried this recipe and fell in love with it.

You can also substitute Asiago for Parmesan in this recipe
for a slightly sharper taste.

Total Prep Time: 20 minutes

Yield: 4

Ingredient List:

- 8 ounces onion, thinly sliced
- ½ peeled and seeded butternut squash, sliced thin
- 1 tsp. rosemary, chopped
- A pinch of salt and black pepper
- 1 ½ ounces extra-virgin olive oil, divided
- All –purpose flour
- 16 ounces refrigerated pizza crust dough, divided
- ½ ounce cornmeal
- 1 ounce Parmesan cheese, grated

HHHHHHHHHHHHHHHHHHHHHHHHHHHHHHHHHHHHHHHH

Instructions:

1. Preheat oven to 400 degrees Fahrenheit

2. Arrange onion and squash in a roasting pan and season with salt, pepper, rosemary and 1 ounce of olive oil. Mix until vegetables are completely coated

3. Bake pan in oven for 20 minutes or until vegetables are tender. Remove from heat and set aside

4. Turn the oven up to 450 degrees Fahrenheit

5. Sprinkle flour on a flat surface and start to roll dough into small balls

6. Flatten the balls into small rounds of 8" in diameter

7. Take a large baking sheet and sprinkle with cornmeal

8. Put the dough rounds on the baking sheet, giving ample space between each round

9. Add the vegetable mixture from the roasting pan to the rounds evenly and bake for 10 minutes or until crust is golden brown and crispy

10. Remove from heat and top with cheese and the rest of the olive oil

11. Cut into pieces and serve

Recipe 17: Tomatoless Pizza

The sour cream and cream cheese make this one of the creamiest pizzas you will find in this recipe book. I would recommend using the freshest vegetables you can purchase to get the most out of this natural and healthy dish.

Total Prep Time: 15 minutes

Yield: 4

Ingredient List:

- 10 ounces refrigerated pizza crust dough
- 8 ounces light sour cream
- 8 ounces softened cream cheese
- 1 tsp. dill weed, dried
- ½ ounce olive oil
- 6 sliced fresh mushrooms
- 1 peeled onion, sliced
- 1 minced clove of garlic
- ½ seeded red bell pepper, sliced into thin strips
- 6 ounces baby spinach leaves

HHHHHHHHHHHHHHHHHHHHHHHHHHHHHHHHHHHHHH

Instructions:

1. Preheat the oven to 375 degrees Fahrenheit

2. Spray a baking sheet with cooking spray and then spread the pizza dough out, pressing down to cover the whole sheet

3. Combine the sour cream, cream cheese and dill in a medium sized bowl until the mixture is smooth and creamy

4. Spread the mix from the bowl evenly over the pizza crust

5. Heat oil in a large frying pan on medium heat

6. Stir in onion, mushrooms, garlic and peppers and cook for 4 minutes or until onion is translucent and tender. Stop just before the pepper gets soft.

7. Add spinach and remove from heat

8. Spread the mixture from the pan over the pizza and bake for 15 minutes or until crust is golden brown

Recipe 18: Ranch Pizza

This recipe is one 'meaty' vegetarian pizza and comes with many different fresh vegetables that are healthy and tasty. The ranch dressing is a unique flavor that makes an excellent substitute for tomato sauce.

Total Prep Time: 20 minutes

Yield: 10

Ingredient List:

- 12" uncooked pizza crust
- 12 ounces Ranch dressing
- 16 ounces Cheddar cheese, shredded
- 4 ounces carrots, shredded
- 4 ounces cauliflower, chopped
- 4 ounces fresh broccoli, chopped
- 4 ounces onion, chopped
- 4 ounces red bell pepper, chopped
- 4 ounces fresh mushrooms, sliced
- 16 ounces shredded mozzarella cheese

HHHHHHHHHHHHHHHHHHHHHHHHHHHHHHHHHHHHHHHH

Instructions:

1. Preheat oven to 350 degrees Fahrenheit

2. Put pizza crust on a large baking sheet or pizza pan and evenly cover with Ranch dressing

3. Top dressing with the rest of the Ingredients in any order you choose except for the mozzarella cheese, which should go on last

4. Bake for 20 minutes or until cheese is melted and vegetables are soft

Recipe 19: Sweet Potato and Lentil Pizza

This recipe has a unique mixture of non-traditional pizza vegetables such as lentils, sweet potatoes, and eggplant. The consistency is chunky, making this one of the heartiest pizzas you will ever make without meat.

Total Prep Time: 30 minutes

Yield: 8

Ingredient List:

- 6 ounces dry red lentils
- 12 ounces water
- ½ ounce extra-virgin olive oil
- 2 minced cloves garlic
- 1 chopped onion
- ½ diced eggplant
- 16 ounces cubed sweet potato
- 14 ½ ounces canned Italian-style diced tomatoes, with liquid
- 1 tsp. ginger, ground
- 1 ½ tsp. curry powder
- ½ ounce cumin, ground
- A pinch of salt and pepper
- 12" prebaked whole wheat pizza crust, thin crust
- 2 ounces Romano cheese, grated

HHHHHHHHHHHHHHHHHHHHHHHHHHHHHHHHHHHHHHHH

Instructions:

1. In a small pan, mix lentils and water and bring to a boil. Cover the pan and simmer on Low heat until tender. This should take about 20 minutes

2. Remove from heat, drain the water and set the pan aside

3. Preheat the oven to 375 degrees Fahrenheit

4. Coat a large baking sheet with cooking spray or oil and set aside

5. Heat olive oil in a large frying pan on medium heat

6. Sauté garlic and onions until garlic is tender and onion is translucent

7. Add eggplant, sweet potato and 4 ounces of the juice from the tomatoes

8. Simmer the mixture until the liquid evaporates

9. Add tomatoes, ginger, curry, cumin, salt and pepper

10. Continue to cook for 20 minutes or until sweet potatoes are tender

11. Put the pizza crust on a baking sheet or pizza pan

12. Spread lentil mixture evenly over the top, then add sweet potatoes over the lentils

13. Top with cheese and bake for 13 minutes or until edges of the crust are slightly browned

Recipe 20: Whole Wheat Pesto Pizza

you are looking for a lower calorie alternative that will give you a generous serving of grains, then this whole wheat pizza will do the trick. I have taken to using whole wheat pizza crust for many pizzas because it is healthier and just as tasty.

Total Prep Time: 20 minutes

Yield: 6

Ingredient List:

- 12" prepared whole-wheat pizza crust
- 8 ounces prepared pesto
- 12 ounces fresh spinach, chopped
- 1 chopped tomato
- 8 ounces mozzarella cheese, shredded
- 4 ounces feta cheese, crumbled

HHHHHHHHHHHHHHHHHHHHHHHHHHHHHHHHHHHHHHHH

Instructions:

1. Preheat oven to 450 degrees Fahrenheit

2. Put pizza crust on a large baking sheet and spread the pesto evenly over the top

3. Add the rest of the Ingredients in layers, ending with the feta and mozzarella cheese

4. Bake for 12 minutes or until cheese has been melted and the crust is golden brown

Recipe 21: Basil Goat Cheese Pizza

This recipe uses bread dough as opposed to traditional pizza crust which tastes just as delicious. It is always better to bake the dough first before placing the toppings, so the base is slightly cooked and doesn't absorb a lot of liquid and get mushy.

Total Prep Time: 10 minutes

Yield: 4

Ingredient List:

- 16 ounce loaf thawed frozen white bread dough
- All-purpose flour
- ½ ounce extra-virgin olive oil
- A pinch of salt
- ½ tsp. black pepper, ground
- 3 chopped sprigs of basil, divided
- 1 ½ tsp. rosemary, minced
- 6 ounces Italian seasoned tomato sauce
- 4 ounces goat cheese, crumbled

HHHHHHHHHHHHHHHHHHHHHHHHHHHHHHHHHHHHHHH

Instructions:

1. Put the dough in a bowl covered with plastic wrap until it rises to double the original size

2. Preheat oven to 425 degrees Fahrenheit

3. Sprinkle flour on a flat surface and roll the dough out into a 16" round

4. Roll the edges of the round towards the centre until the dough resembles a pizza crust

5. Lightly brush crust with oil and season with salt, pepper, 1 chopped sprig of basil and rosemary

6. Bake for 10 minutes or until crust is golden brown

7. Remove from heat and spread the tomato sauce evenly over the crust

8. Add the rest of the basil and sprinkle with goat cheese

9. Bake for another 8 minutes or until heated through

Recipe 22: Vegetable Dill Pizza

Dill is a natural seasoning to use when it comes to most vegetarian pizza recipes. This dish uses crescent roll dough that is soft, chewy and scrumptious.

Total Prep Time: 25 minutes

Yield: 16

Ingredient List:

- Cooking spray
- 8 ounces refrigerated crescent rolls
- 8 ounces sour cream
- 8 ounces softened cream cheese
- 1 tsp. dill weed, dried
- ¼ tsp. garlic salt
- 1 ounce dry ranch dressing mix
- 1 finely chopped onion,
- 1 thinly sliced stalk of celery
- 4 ounces radishes, sliced thin
- 1 chopped red bell pepper
- 12 ounces fresh chopped broccoli
- 1 grated carrot

HHHHHHHHHHHHHHHHHHHHHHHHHHHHHHHHHHHHHH

Instructions:

1. Preheat oven to 350 degrees Fahrenheit

2. Coat a jellyroll pan with cooking spray

3. Arrange the crescent roll dough in the pan and set aside for 5 minutes

4. Take a fork and poke holes in the dough

5. Bake the dough for 10 minutes or until it turns golden brown

6. Remove from heat and let it cool for 10 minutes

7. Combine sour cream, cream cheese, dill, garlic and ranch dressing mix in a large bowl.

8. Spread the mixture from the bowl evenly on the crescent roll crust

9. Add the rest of the Ingredients to the sour cream mix, cover and chill in refrigerator for ½ hour

10. Cut into small squares and serve

Recipe 23: Pizza Sandwiches

This recipe is a healthy alternative to the pizza pops or wraps that you would ordinarily find in the grocery store. The crescent roll dough is soft and easily molded into a delicious sandwich shaped pizza.

Total Prep Time: 10 minutes

Yield: 4

Ingredient List:

- 8 ounces refrigerated crescent rolls
- 4 slices mozzarella cheese
- ½ ounce tomato paste
- ½ tsp. oregano, dried

HHHHHHHHHHHHHHHHHHHHHHHHHHHHHHHHHHHHHHH

Instructions:

1. Preheat oven to 350 degrees Fahrenheit

2. Spread crescent roll dough on a flat surface and separate into 4 rectangles

3. Place two rectangles on a large baking sheet and sprinkle water on the edges of to moisten

4. On each rectangle, arrange 2 slices of mozzarella and tomato paste

5. Sprinkle oregano over the paste and then close the pizza with the other half of the dough. Press the edges closed to seal firmly

6. Bake for 12 minutes or until outer crust is golden brown

Recipe 24: Sun-Dried Tomato Pizza

The jalapeno peppers in this recipe give this pizza a subtle heat that complements the sun-dried tomatoes ground into the pesto. I like to serve this with some jalapeno jelly for dipping when I serve this as an appetizer.

Total Prep Time: 15 minutes

Yield: 8

Ingredient List:

- 1 ounce melted butter
- ½ ounce extra-virgin olive oil
- 1 ½ ounces garlic, minced
- 1 ounce sun-dried tomato pesto
- 1 tsp. basil leaves, dried
- 1 tsp. oregano, dried
- ½ ounce Parmesan cheese, grated
- 12" uncooked pizza crust
- 1 sliced tomato
- 1 bunch fresh spinach, torn into small pieces
- 1 sliced sweet onion
- 1 chopped jalapeno pepper,
- 6 ounces crumbled feta cheese

HHHHHHHHHHHHHHHHHHHHHHHHHHHHHHHHHHHHHHHHHH

Instructions:

1. According to the temperature on the package of pizza crust, set the oven to preheat

2. Combine oil, butter, garlic, sun-dried tomato pesto, basil, oregano and Parmesan in a small bowl

3. Spread the oil mixture evenly over the pizza crust

4. Add onion, tomato and jalapeno pepper to the oil mixture and then top with feta

5. Bake for 10-15 minutes or until the cheese has been melted and the crust is golden brown

Recipe 25: Arugula and Hummus Pizza

This recipe is a tasty and light snack perfect for appetizers if cut into small squares or wedges. The hummus makes a creamy base for the arugula and complements the sour bite of the balsamic vinegar.

Total Prep Time: 10 minutes

Yield: 1

Ingredient List:

- 1 ounce hummus
- 1 naan bread
- 8 ounces arugula
- 1 pitted date, finely chopped
- 1 ounce pumpkin seeds
- 1 tsp. balsamic vinegar

HHHHHHHHHHHHHHHHHHHHHHHHHHHHHHHHHHHHH

Instructions:

Put naan on a serving dish and spread the hummus evenly over the top

Arrange arugula, chopped date, and pumpkin seeds on the hummus

Drizzle vinegar over the bread and serve

Recipe 26: Broccoli and Cauliflower Pizza

If your kids don't want to eat their vegetables, then try serving them on this chewy and tasty pizza recipe. The broccoli and cauliflower create a healthy meal that the family will love while also giving them their necessary veggies.

Total Prep Time: 30 minutes

Yield: 12

Ingredient List:

- 8 ounces refrigerated crescent rolls
- 8 ounces softened cream cheese
- 8 ounces mayonnaise
- 1 ounce dry Ranch salad dressing mix
- 8 ounces chopped broccoli
- 8 ounces tomatoes, chopped
- 8 ounces green bell pepper, chopped
- 8 ounces cauliflower, chopped
- 8 ounces carrots, shredded
- 8 ounces Cheddar cheese, shredded

HHHHHHHHHHHHHHHHHHHHHHHHHHHHHHHHHHHHHH

Instructions:

1. Preheat oven to 375 degrees Fahrenheit

2. On a large baking sheet, roll the crescent roll dough out and pinch the edges to make a pizza crust

3. Bake crescent roll dough for 12 minutes or until golden brown

4. Remove from heat and set it aside for 15 minutes to cool

5. Combine cream cheese, Ranch mix and mayonnaise in a small bowl

6. Spread the cream cheese mix evenly over the pizza crust

7. Layer the vegetables on the cream cheese and then sprinkle with cheddar

8. Put the pizza in the refrigerator for 1 hour and then cut in small squares and serve

Recipe 27: Pita Pizza with Pesto

This pita pizza is a refreshing change from the usual heavy crust, and pita bread is also much easier to bake. These mini-pizzas are fun to make and eat for children because they are individual-sized.

Total Prep Time: 15 minutes

Yield: 4

Ingredient List:

- 4 pita bread rounds
- 4 ounces pesto
- 2 sliced tomatoes
- 4 ounces feta cheese, crumbled

HHHHHHHHHHHHHHHHHHHHHHHHHHHHHHHHHHHHHHHH

Instructions:

1. Preheat oven to 375 degrees Fahrenheit

2. Put pitas on a large baking sheet and bake for 5 minutes or until slightly toasted

3. Remove from heat and spread the pesto over each pita round evenly,

4. Arrange tomato over the pesto and then top each round with feta cheese

5. Bake for 10 minutes or until pita bread is crisp

Recipe 28: Hummus Pizza

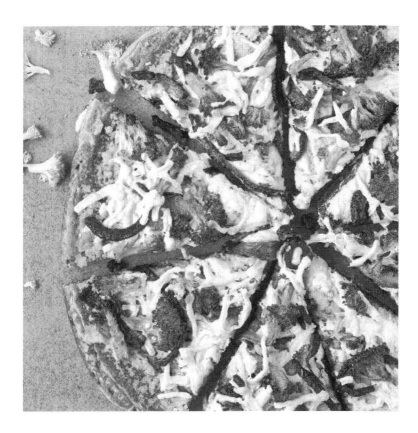

The hummus in this recipe creates a creamy texture that melts in your mouth with each bite. I especially like the taste of the Monterey Jack cheese in place of traditional mozzarella in this dish because it has a refreshing flavor.

Total Prep Time: 15 minutes

Yield: 8

Ingredient List:

- 10 ounces refrigerated pizza crust dough
- 8 ounces hummus
- 12 ounces red bell peppers, sliced
- 8 ounces broccoli florets
- 16 ounces Monterey Jack cheese, shredded

HHHHHHHHHHHHHHHHHHHHHHHHHHHHHHHHHHHHHHHH

Instructions:

1. Preheat the oven to 475 degrees Fahrenheit

2. On a large pizza pan, roll the crust out and spread the hummus evenly over the top

3. Add peppers and broccoli over the hummus and then sprinkle with cheese

4. Bake for 15 minutes or until crust is golden brown and cheese is melted

Recipe 29: Sundried Tomato and Onion Pizza

This recipe is another one that uses goat cheese as a lovely addition to the traditional pizza Ingredients. I like to serve this pizza with some red pepper flakes and some extra sun-dried tomatoes on the side.

Total Prep Time: 20 minutes

Yield: 6

Ingredient List:

- 10 ounces refrigerated pizza dough
- 2 ounces olive oil
- 2 minced cloves garlic
- 1 sliced red onion,
- A pinch of salt and black pepper
- 4 ounces sun-dried tomatoes, chopped
- 8 ounces goat cheese, crumbled
- 8 ounces provolone cheese, shredded
- ½ ounce herbes de Provence

HHHHHHHHHHHHHHHHHHHHHHHHHHHHHHHHHHHHHHHHH

Instructions:

1. Preheat oven to 400 degrees Fahrenheit

2. Spray a baking pan with cooking oil

3. Spread pizza dough on the baking pan and flatten

4. Bake for 5 minutes or until a little bit cooked

5. Heat oil in a large frying pan on Medium heat

6. Sauté garlic for 2 minutes or until tender and then add onion

7. Cook for an additional 15 minutes or until onion is translucent

8. Remove pan from heat and sprinkle onions with salt and pepper

9. Lightly brush pizza crust with grease drippings from frying pan

10. Arrange onion, tomatoes, goat cheese and provolone evenly over pizza

11. Season with herbes de Provence and bake for 15 minutes or until cheese has been melted and the crust is golden brown

Recipe 30: Onion and Gorgonzola Pizza

There will rarely be a slice left of this pizza when it is served with a meal or as an appetizer. The onion and blue cheese mix well, and the result is creamy and delicious, not to mention addictive.

Total Prep Time: 15 minutes

Yield: 12

Ingredient List:

- 1 ounce butter
- 2 thinly sliced Vidalia onions,
- 2 tsp. sugar
- 10 ounces package refrigerated pizza dough
- 16 ounces of crumbled Gorgonzola cheese

HHHHHHHHHHHHHHHHHHHHHHHHHHHHHHHHHHHHHHH

Instructions:

1. Melt butter in a large frying pan on medium heat

2. Sauté onions for 25 minutes or until they are dark brown

3. Add sugar and cook for another 2 minutes

4. Preheat oven to 425 degrees Fahrenheit

5. Coat a baking sheet or pizza pan with cooking spray and roll the pizza dough out to the edges or to the desired size and thickness

6. Arrange onions on the crust and sprinkle with cheese

7. Bake for 12 minutes or until cheese melts

About the Author

Angel Burns learned to cook when she worked in the local seafood restaurant near her home in Hyannis Port in Massachusetts as a teenager. The head chef took Angel under his wing and taught the young woman the tricks of the trade for cooking seafood. The skills she had learned at a young age helped her get accepted into Boston University's Culinary Program where she also minored in business administration.

Summers off from school meant working at the same restaurant but when Angel's mentor and friend retired as head chef, she took over after graduation and created classic and new dishes that delighted the diners. The restaurant flourished under Angel's culinary creativity and one customer developed more than an appreciation for Angel's food. Several months after taking over the position, the young woman met her future husband at work and they have been inseparable ever since. They still live in Hyannis Port with their two children and a cocker spaniel named Buddy.

Angel Burns turned her passion for cooking and her business acumen into a thriving e-book business. She has authored several successful books on cooking different types of dishes using simple ingredients for novices and experienced chefs alike. She is still head chef in Hyannis Port and says she will probably never leave!

Author's Afterthoughts

With so many books out there to choose from, I want to thank you for choosing this one and taking precious time out of your life to buy and read my work. Readers like you are the reason I take such passion in creating these books.

It is with gratitude and humility that I express how honored I am to become a part of your life and I hope that you take the same pleasure in reading this book as I did in writing it.

Can I ask one small favour? I ask that you write an honest and open review on Amazon of what you thought of the book. This will help other readers make an informed choice on whether to buy this book.

My sincerest thanks,

Angel Burns

If you want to be the first to know about news, new books, events and giveaways, subscribe to my newsletter by clicking the link below

https://angel-burns.gr8.com

or Scan QR-code

Printed in Great Britain
by Amazon